WHAT MRS. EDDY SAID
TO
ARTHUR BRISBANE

NOTE: This book contains six authentic pictures of
Mary Baker Eddy.

MARY BAKER EDDY

From a painting by
Alice H. Barbour

WHAT MRS. EDDY SAID
TO
ARTHUR BRISBANE

The Celebrated Interview of the Eminent
Journalist With the Discoverer and
Founder of Christian Science

The Mother Church
Erected 1894

1930

M. E. PAIGE, Publisher
33 WEST FORTY-SECOND STREET :: NEW YORK

.

Printed in the United States of America by
J. J. LITTLE AND IVES COMPANY, NEW YORK

INTRODUCTION

ARTHUR BRISBANE, the eminent American writer and editor, published an article in the Cosmopolitan Magazine in August, 1907, which was destined to become an historic document among those interested, as faithful adherents or merely as students of important events of their times, in Christian Science.

The article was a vivid pen picture of Mary Baker Eddy as she appeared in that year, mentally, physically and spiritually, and because of a press dispute over her condition and circumstances, the establishing of the facts concerning Mrs. Eddy was of the utmost significance.

The interview became famous. The Cosmopolitan Magazine printed and sold out a large edition of that issue. The interview was later published in book form and numerous editions were absorbed by the reading public. The fact that the well-known writer of the interview was avowedly not a Christian Scientist, and therefore not subject to a conscious or unconscious

prejudice in favor of his subject, added weight
to his statements.

The document had a profound meaning for
interested observers of Christian Science as a
major religious movement; while to adherents
of the faith the interview meant confirmation
beyond question of fundamental statements that
were being made by and on behalf of their
Leader. Now after almost a quarter of a century
the noted article is viewed as having lost neither
in interest nor in meaning. To the historical stu-
dent it is still a guide-post in his search for the
truth; while to the Christian Scientist it is in the
nature of a heritage perhaps beyond price.

A demand for copies on the part of members
and friends of the Christian Science Church
would seem sufficient justification for publish-
ing the interview anew in this book, yet there
is a more impelling reason in that a new edition is necessary to meet the needs of historical
record. And there is an additional consideration.
As history demonstrates only too well, untruthful
attacks upon great religious leaders have been
unmasked and defeated in one generation only
to be renewed with all the original pretenses in
the next; and thus these celebrated statements

THE FIRST CHURCH OF CHRIST SCIENTIST, BOSTON, MASSACHUSETTS

by a celebrated and disinterested writer may be of as much service in the future as they were in 1907 in allaying falsehoods and establishing the facts regarding an outstanding world figure.

Christian Science consistently undertakes, instead of exalting person, to substitute what it denominates as Principle for personality; yet in the matter of this interview the personal condition and circumstances of Mary Baker Eddy became of rightful concern to the world because, inevitably, they would argue for or against the truth of the teachings upon which she had founded the Church of Christ, Scientist. In fact, in giving the public a picture of Mrs. Eddy exactly as she was when he visited her, Mr. Brisbane was providing readers of that generation and of future generations with a lens through which they might better judge the things Mrs. Eddy had presented as having come to her in divine revelation.

To perpetuate the Brisbane interview, and not to add to it, is the purpose of this book; yet a plain need is the justification of this introductory statement. Mr. Brisbane set at rest issues which had been raised, designedly and sensationally, in the public mind. He answered, di-

rectly and by implication, questions which were
so well known then as to need no repetition by
him; but the reader of today will better understand and appreciate if there is placed before
him in brief résumé the affairs and conditions
provoking the questions to which Mr. Brisbane,
in effect, replied.

The year 1907 was to prove momentous and
unforgettable in the annals of Christian Science.
It was to usher in continued and bitter attacks.
These assaults were not to be logical sallies
against the precepts of the new and fast-grow-
ing religion, but were to seek its retardation and
destruction by personal attacks upon its Leader,
Mrs. Eddy—attacks startling in their viciousness
and, as it developed, in the lengths to which mis-
representation might be carried. The halting and
dissipating of the Christian Science Cause was
apparently what its enemies desired, but they
sought to accomplish their ends by traducing the
Leader. If she fell, her church might hardly be
expected to prosper thereafter.

Christian Science was reaching the end of its
first generation. Its textbook, Science and Health
with Key to the Scriptures, by Mrs. Eddy, had
been in print thirty years and had gone through

many large editions. The movement appeared to some of its enemies like a swiftly-grown mushroom which a determined heel could crush out of the path. The attack, initiated by a small group, was joined by other agencies in such numbers and with such energy that, seemingly, only a thing based upon a foundation as substantial as that to which it professed could have withstood the storm. When innuendo, satire and malice loosed their bolts through the public press there was an early and unexpected rallying to the defense by persons who held no official relation to the movement but who were actuated strongly by the springs of justice or personal gratitude. Many printed onslaughts and many printed defenses were followed by an attempt in the courts by persons styling themselves the "next friends" of Mrs. Eddy to take over the control of her extensive estate as well as her person.

Thus the year 1907 witnessed, in the newspapers and magazines and the courts of law, the fullest airing of the teachings and fruitage of Christian Science and of the bodily health, mental activity and outlook upon life and men of Mary Baker Eddy. The spring of the year saw

the onslaught at its height; the summer saw the
faithful defenders rallying to the support of the
Cause; the fall saw the downfall of the legal
attack upon the person and estate of Mrs. Eddy,
and the year closed with the press generally,
whatever the opinions of the editors regarding
Christian Science as a religion, declaring that
the Cause had gone through a crisis and had
emerged in the glow of a complete and fully-
earned victory.

The attacks on Mrs. Eddy were initiated by
certain newspapers in the fall of 1906. In sen-
sational, unauthenticated articles they referred
to her at the age of 85 as incapable of handling
her own affairs and as suffering with "senile
debility", "mental infirmity" and "physical in-
capacity"—three rounded terms which were to
be seized upon and used again and again by
unfriendly writers and to be repeated in a court
document when the "next friends" sought to take
over her person and estate.

In its issue of December, 1906, McClure's
Magazine announced a series of "unbiased" articles and used the following paragraph, which
took on added significance when it was found

INTERIOR VIEW OF THE FIRST CHURCH OF CHRIST SCIENTIST, BOSTON, MASSACHÚSETTS

that the articles were anything but friendly in their attitude:

"In 1875 ten or twelve disciples of one Mary Baker Glover, teacher of a system of healing disease by the mind, met at Lynn, Massachusetts, organized by resolution the first Christian Scientist Association, and pledged ten dollars a week for the support of Mary Glover as their teacher. In June, 1906, Christian Scientists of the world met in Boston to dedicate the most costly church building in New England and one of the most pretentious in the United States; for in thirty-one years the Association had grown into a Church, and the Church into six hundred churches. In 1875 no one living outside of two or three back streets of Lynn had heard of Christian Science. Now, the very name is a catch phrase. In those early days the leader and teacher paid one-half of her ten dollars a week to hire a hall, patching out the rest of her living with precarious fees as an instructor in mental healing; now, she is one of the richest women in the United States. She is more than that—she is the most powerful American woman."

The magazine said of Mrs. Eddy: "Her isolation is now like that of the Grand Lama," and in its opening article, by way of showing that Mrs. Eddy was more aged in appearance than her followers had been led to believe, published a portrait which had no resemblance to Mrs. Eddy, but which was soon identified as that of an elderly lady living in Brooklyn.

While some newspapers were declaring that the author of the Christian Science textbook, Science and Health with Key to the Scriptures, was "doddering with age" and being misused by persons close to her, Herbert W. Horwill, in a review of the textbook, of which 366,000 copies had been published, in the London Quarterly Review said: "The leaders of the English churches have not as yet taken into serious account the spread of the Christian Science movement. . . . The new cult has commonly been regarded as merely one of the many strange exhalations that have arisen from the peculiar soil of the United States." The article, which was critical and unfriendly to a degree, contained this paragraph: "Newspaper editors, as a rule, are shrewd judges of the public mind, and the fact that a paper like the London Tribune should have thought it worth while to publish a verbatim report of a long lecture by Mr. Bicknell

MRS. EDDY ABOUT 1868

Young in the Albert Hall is a notable evidence
of the success of the Christian Science propa-
ganda in arresting general attention. We may as
well admit that, as Mrs. Eddy's compatriots
would put it, Christian Science has 'come to
stay', and not only to stay, but for some time
at least to grow."

The Monist was one of several magazines
which, taking note of the general hubbub being
raised over the subject, sought to explain away
Christian Science on the ground that it presented
nothing new. "The Christian Science movement
is a revival of a belief based upon certain expe-
riences and to some extent justified by remarkable events that have happened again and again
under all zones and in all ages," averred the
Monist. "Such beliefs crop out spontaneously
whenever they are needed and will disappear
again when they have done their work. . . .
But to those who lack the self-discipline which
ought to be a part of an all-round education, it
(the gospel of Christian Science) will come as
a remarkable help in many difficult situations
and will, if it be but kept within fair limits, con-
tribute to their spiritual as well as bodily wel-
fare."

This article by the editor of the Monist was
called forth, apparently, by one appearing in
that magazine from the pen of E. T. Brewster,
who reached the conclusion that, "The real
reason why at the present moment Christian Science is spreading by leaps and bounds is that,
all theory aside, it does make men and women
happy. Its one clear call is that

'The mind is its own place
And of itself can make a Heaven of Hell,
A Hell of Heaven.' "

The flood of bitter ridicule and misrepresenta-
tion that was running in a certain stratum of the
newspaper press caused to appear as champions
in the pages of the magazines prominent persons
whose interest in Christian Science had not been
a matter of common knowledge.

Frederick W. Root, the composer, writing in
the Fine Arts Journal, said: "Christian Science
seems to appeal rather strongly to musicians,
more forcibly perhaps than to those engaged in
other occupations. . . . The musician is perhaps less hampered than others by a stolid ma-
terialism. The subject with which he occupies
himself is largely idealistic; and his profes-

TAKEN AT LYNN, MASS., ABOUT 1868. THIS PICTURE WAS SNAPPED FOR THE MOTHER, FOR WHOM MRS. EDDY HAD CALMED THE CHILD SO THAT ITS PORTRAIT MIGHT BE MADE. NOTE THE EXPRESSION OF MRS. EDDY'S EYES

sional success is manifestly a question of consciousness rather than of matter. Naturally, then, whatever teaches a science of Mind that proves as fruitful of good results as does Christian Science, is attractive to him."

Clara Louise Burnham, the novelist, wrote in the February issue of The World Today: "I, too, covered valuable paper with exhortations to misguided relatives and friends who had been inexplicably caught in the meshes of what I hotly detested as a false transcendentalism. . . . It was physical misery which faithful physicians could not relieve that forced me to turn to Christian Science. I was healed; and the help came so suddenly that it shocked me out of my intention to withdraw at the first possible moment from its influence. Under the permeating goodness, purity and truth of the new teaching, one after another of the conditions which hampered my life slipped away, and I stood forth a free being."

The favoring article by a prominent layman which caused the widest comment was one written by Charles Klein, author of "The Music Master," "The Lion and the Mouse" and other well-known dramas. The February Cosmopolitan in which it appeared sold out an edition of 450,000 copies, then an unprecedented printing for that magazine, and the business manager stated that 75,000 additional copies could have been sold had they been available.

"The articles on Christian Science which are appearing from day to day in the public journals and magazines," Mr. Klein wrote, "throw very little light on the subject because, for the most part, these articles are written by persons who have made only a superficial investigation of that science or have submitted it to no personal test, relying largely on one-sided testimony, casual, critical observation,.or on the say-so of members of other religious denominations, schools of medicine, etc., who may or may not be more or less prejudiced against it. It is the personal test, and that only, which enables a man to become an authoritative judge of the reasonableness of the claims of Christian Science."

Mr. Klein supplied the following graphic picture of Mrs. Eddy: "In appearance she seems to be rather tall and dignified, almost stately. As a matter of fact, she is not very tall, but she has the most impressive manner of any person I have ever met. It is an innate, dominating spir-

MRS. EDDY IN 1880, HOLDING IN HER HANDS A COPY OF
THE FIRST EDITION OF SCIENCE AND HEALTH WITH KEY
TO THE SCRIPTURES

itual individuality that asserts itself almost without effort. Her voice is the voice of one who knows, and not of one who merely believes. There is no hysterical gush, no fanatic spirit of ecstasy, but a calm, self-possessed, well-poised mental equilibrium that is remarkable in a woman of her years. That one endowed with such extraordinary executive ability in organization, the most resourceful writer of the day on metaphysical questions, should still retain her mental grasp on the world's affairs is in itself a tribute to the efficacy of the Science she discovered."

Mr. Klein met the charge that Mrs. Eddy was "as isolated as the Grand Lama" by saying: "Mrs. Eddy seeks seclusion, and for a good reason. Like all thinkers, she must spend a great deal of time in meditation, that is, in mental work. There is nothing mystical or mysterious about her solitude. She is really no more inaccessible than the head of any big enterprise."

Besides Mr. Brisbane, William E. Curtis, the noted correspondent of the Chicago Record-Herald, Edwin J. Park of the Boston Globe, and Sibyl Wilbur, whose life of Mrs. Eddy appeared first in Human Life Magazine, did not find Mrs.

Eddy inaccessible. Mr. Curtis and Mr. Park wrote entertainingly in their journals of their visits with her and of their observations of her mental keenness and spiritual perception.

After Mrs. Eddy had been examined by a special commission and noted alienists on behalf of the Court and their findings had brought about the collapse of the "next friends" suit, the New York American said: "The assertion that Mrs. Eddy, old and doddering, had fallen into the hands of designing men and women who sought to use her to further their own purposes, is thus proved to be as baseless as the numerous reports of her death which have been made from time to time by enemies of her religion."

After quoting editorial comment from several leading newspapers, and noting a general opinion that the suit had been an attack on religious freedom, the Literary Digest thus summed up the events of an exciting year: "In this connection it is interesting to note the change that has taken place in the prevailing attitude of the press toward Christian Science. A little while ago the papers seemed to regard the subject chiefly as a target for their ridicule, whereas

MRS. EDDY'S HOME IN LYNN, MASSACHUSETTS

now the comment, even where hostile, is respect-
ful."

Among the writers who turned their pens to
the subject of Christian Science and Mary Baker
Eddy in that momentous year of 1907 came the
distinguished Arthur Brisbane. None could have
been more ably qualified for the performance of
a piece of journalistic work that was to produce
a profound effect upon the public mind and to
endure as a living page that would reflect things
of importance to the future. Mr. Brisbane was
born in Buffalo. He was educated in the American public schools and then spent five years in
study in France and Germany. He began his
newspaper career as a reporter on the New York
Sun in December, 1883. After serving as London correspondent of his paper, he returned to
become managing editor of the Evening Sun.
He was editor of the New York World for seven
years, became editor of the New York Evening
Journal in 1897 and ever since has remained
an editor of the Hearst group of newspapers.
Through his daily editorial "Today", appearing
in a large number of newspapers throughout the
country, he is said to reach more readers regu-
larly than any other living writer.

Himself not a Christian Scientist, Mr. Brisbane brought to the important and exacting task of presenting an absolutely just portrait of Mrs. Eddy as she then was to the world the powers of a trained journalistic mind as free from bias as from careless observation and indefinite expression. This somewhat extended introduction has been provided in order that, by grasping the circumstances of the time and undertaking, the reader may better understand and appreciate an absorbingly interesting interview which was regarded as a masterstroke in the day of its original publication and which today can hardly be regarded as other than a living beacon to light the path of inquirers no less interested than were their fathers.

RUFUS STEELE

AN INTERVIEW WITH MRS. EDDY

GRAPHIC DESCRIPTION OF THE PHYSICAL AND MENTAL CONDITION OF THE VENERABLE FOUNDER OF CHRISTIAN SCIENCE AT HER CONCORD HOME ON THE EIGHTH OF JUNE, 1907.

By Arthur Brisbane

(EDITOR'S NOTE: The following article was written by Arthur Brisbane at the special request of the Cosmopolitan Magazine. The fact that Mr. Brisbane is not and never has been a believer in Christian Science gives added value to his statements as to Mrs. Eddy's clear thought and sound health.)

WHERE there is a big effect there is a big cause. When you see flame, lava, and dust coming up from the mouth of Vesuvius, you know there is power below the crater.

When you see millions savagely fighting in the name of one leader, or patiently submissive and gentle in the name of another, you know that there was power. in those men.

When you see tens of thousands of modern, enlightened human beings absolutely devoted to the teachings of Mrs. Eddy, their leader, and beyond all question made happy and contented by her teachings, you know there is a cause underlying that wonderful effect.

Millions of people in this country will be interested in the personality of the very remarkable woman who founded Christian Science, and gathered together the great Christian Science following.

This is written to describe an interview with Mrs. Eddy which took place in her house at Concord, New Hampshire, at about two o'clock in the afternoon of Saturday, June 8th.

Carlyle would not forgive the old monk who talked to the medieval English king on his travels and then failed to describe the king accurately and in detail. The first duty of a writer who sees a personality interesting to the world is to tell what he has seen, rather than what he thinks. For what one man has seen another would see, whereas one does not think what another thinks.

Mrs. Eddy's house at Concord is extremely simple and unpretentious, a plain, little frame

MRS. EDDY ADDRESSING GUESTS—PLEASANT VIEW

dwelling, situated rather close to a country road-
way on the side of a most beautiful New Hampshire valley. The view from her windows is
across this valley to the blue hills. Behind those
hills, a very few miles distant, is the spot where
Mrs. Eddy was born.

Mrs. Eddy's thought has spread all around
this world. It has found expression in heavy
stone churches and great audiences from Maine
to California, and across the oceans. This distant
work her mind has done; her frail body dwells
in peace and quiet in the simplest, most modest
of homes, almost on the spot where her physical
life began.

Around the frame dwelling runs a broad
veranda. And above are balconies on which Mrs.
Eddy sits or stands, looking down to the minia-
ture lake dug with the contributions of men and
women deeply grateful to her, or across the wide
fields toward the city and the busy world to
which she voluntarily said good-bye long ago.

The house is furnished very plainly. In the
room on the right of the entrance the chief orna-
ment is a large illuminated hymnal presented
by the Earl of Dunmore, one of Mrs. Eddy's
British followers. In that room and in the room

on the left of the entrance the furniture is extremely simple. There are a few pictures, and on one of the walls is a bas-relief of Mrs. Eddy in white marble.

These rooms downstairs are kept scrupulously neat. They are evidently used rarely. Mrs. Eddy occupies almost exclusively her living-rooms one flight above.

The home of the Christian Science leader has been called by writers of strong imagination "A House of Mystery."

As a matter of fact, the house is about as mysterious as the average little New England home. It could be reproduced, furniture and all, for a good deal less than ten thousand dollars. All the doors, downstairs and upstairs, are open. It is the very peaceful, quiet abode of an old lady tenderly cared for by devoted women, earnest followers of Mrs. Eddy's teachings. These Christian Science ladies, who greeted the writer at the top of a narrow flight of stairs, were not in any way different from ordinary women, except that all three had very peaceful, happy expressions. Among three ordinary women, you usually find one or two whose expressions make you feel sorry for them.

HOUSE FROM DAISY FIELD—PLEASANT VIEW

These devoted friends of Mrs. Eddy were dressed very plainly, in light, cotton gowns. And they seemed as deeply interested and excited about a visitor from the outside world as though they had been three eighteen-year-old schoolgirls watching the arrival of some other girl's brother.

One of them came forward to say, "Mrs. Eddy is very glad that you have come and will see you. Please come into her sitting-room."

She led the way into a corner room at the rear of the house, with wide windows overlooking the valley and the distant hills.

Beside a writing-desk, in an armchair, sat a white-haired woman who rose and walked forward, extending her hand in friendly greeting to a stranger. That was Mrs. Eddy, for whom many human beings in this world feel deepest reverence and affection, and concerning whom others have thought it necessary or excusable to write and to say unkind and untruthful things.

It is quite certain that nobody could see this beautiful and venerable woman and ever again speak of her except in terms of affectionate reverence and sympathy. There are hundreds of thousands of Christian Scientists who would make almost any sacrifice for the privilege of looking upon Mrs. Eddy's face. It is impossible now for her to see many, and it is therefore a duty to make at least an attempt to convey an idea of the impression created by her personality.

Mrs. Eddy is eighty-six years old. Her thick hair, snow-white, curls about her forehead and temples. She is of medium height and very slender. She probably weighs less than one hundred pounds. But her figure is straight as she rises and walks forward. The grasp of her thin hand is firm; the hand does not tremble.

It is hopeless to try to describe a face made very beautiful by age, deep thought, and many years' exercise of great power. The light blue eyes are strong and concentrated in expression. And the sight, as was soon proved, is that of a woman one-half Mrs. Eddy's age.

Mrs. Eddy's face is almost entirely free from wrinkles—the skin is very clear, many a young woman would be proud to have it. The forehead is high and full, and the whole expression of the face combines benevolence with great strength of will. Mrs. Eddy has accumulated power in this world. She possesses it, she exer-

MRS. EDDY AS SHE LOOKED AT THE TIME SHE TAUGHT HER LAST CLASS IN 1898.

cises it, and she knows it. But it is a gentle
power, and it is possessed by a gentle, diffident,
and modest woman.

Women will want to know what Mrs. Eddy
wore. The writer regrets that he cannot tell.
With some women you see the dress; with Mrs.
Eddy you see only the face, the very earnest
eyes, and the beautiful, quiet expression that
only age and thought can give to a human face.
She wore a white lace collar around her neck,
no jewelry of any kind, and a very simple dress.
That much is remembered.

In reporting this interview with Mrs. Eddy,
it must be understood that no attempt is made
to give her words exactly. Every statement at-
tributed to her is her own, but the exact phrase-
ology must not be considered hers. Christian
Science and Christian Scientists have a language
of their own, and any but a stenographic report
of it might be misleading.

M RS. EDDY talked first of her regret that
the farmers about her, and so many others all
over the country, should be disturbed and in-
jured in their prospects and prosperity by the
unseasonable spring weather. The sun happened

to be shining brightly and warmly on the day of
the interview. She spoke of this, of the beautiful
view from her window, of the little boat-house,
the tiny artificial lake, and other evidences of
affection which she owes to her followers.

She spoke simply of her own life and work
and of her absolute happiness in her peaceful surroundings. She smiled pleasantly at the
women who share her home, and who occasionally came to look through the door.

When she was asked to discuss the lawsuit
affecting her, and other matters now in the public mind, she became very earnest, absolutely
concentrated in expression, voice, and choice of
words. She spoke sometimes leaning back in her
chair, with her eyes turned upward, sometimes
leaning forward, replying to questions with
great intensity. She said to one of her friends,
"Please close the door," and then talked fully
on all the business matters that affect her. In
addition to the writer of this article, there was
present General Streeter, Mrs. Eddy's principal
attorney in her legal matters.

Asked why the lawsuit had been started, seeking to take away from her control of her money
and of her actions, Mrs. Eddy replied in a deep,

earnest voice that could easily have been heard all over the biggest of her churches:

"Greed of gold, young man. They are not interested in me, I am sorry to say, but in my money, and in the desire to control that. They say they want to help me. They never tried to help me when I was working hard years ago and when help would have been so welcome."

General Streeter, as counsel for Mrs. Eddy, wished the writer to ascertain, for himself positively, that Mrs. Eddy is thoroughly competent to understand business matters and to manage them. Therefore, detailed questions were asked with an insistence that in the case of a woman of Mrs. Eddy's age would be most unusual and unnecessary.

Mrs. Eddy's mind on all points brought out was perfectly clear, and her answers were instantaneous. She explained in detail how impossible it was for those about her, even if they wished to, to control her or her fortune, and her statements confirmed those which General Streeter had previously made to the writer.

She gave clearly and earnestly her reasons for executing a recent deed of trust by which she has voluntarily given over to three of her most trusted friends the management, so far as is possible, of her material affairs. She explained the character of each of these men, Henry M. Baker, her cousin and a lawyer, Archibald McLellan, the editor of the "Christian Science Journal" and one of her most trusted assistants, and Josiah E. Fernald, of the National State Capital Bank in Concord.

In praising her cousin, a former congressman and at present a member of the legislature, Mrs. Eddy laughingly described him as a very good man "and as honest as any lawyer can be." She laughed more like a young girl than a woman of eighty-six as she said this, looking quizzically at her thoroughly trusted lawyer, General Streeter.

Mrs. Eddy said: "I have entrusted to these three men, so far as I possibly and properly can, the management of my material interests. My constant effort has been to give more and more of my time and thought to that which I consider really important. And I have given to these three men to do for me the worldly work which is of least importance in my eyes."

Mrs. Eddy started to speak of her son, who is made a factor in the legal action against her.

MRS. EDDY'S HOME—CHESTNUT HILL, MASSACHUSETTS

She told how she had once asked him to live with her, saying: "I offered him all that I had except one five-thousand-dollar bond which I meant to reserve for myself. That was long ago, and he would not come to me then." She spoke of her son's entering the army, and the effect that the army life had had upon his character— he was only sixteen years old when he enlisted. There was motherly pride of the ordinary, human kind in her reference to the number of battles in which he had been honorably engaged. But she was obviously much affected by the fact that he had joined the legal action against her. Her eyes filled with tears, her voice became indistinct, and she could not go on. After a while she turned to General Streeter and said, trying to smile, "You know what they say, General, 'A mother is a mother all her life; a father is a father till he gets a new wife.' "

Mrs. Eddy's discussion of her business matters lasted for at least half an hour. There was no sign of weakness of mind, voice, or body. The quality of Mrs. Eddy's voice is really extraordinary. The writer picked up a periodical, the "Christian Science Journal" for June, 1907, just issued, and asked Mrs. Eddy to read from it, having heard of the quality of her voice which had done so much in influencing her following long ago. It was the writer who selected at random the following extract from page 169, read aloud by Mrs. Eddy:

"THE skeptical and unbelieving may shake their heads and ask with Nicodemus, 'How can these things be?' But the sick who have been healed, the sorrowing who have been comforted, and the sinning who have been saved, can look up and answer in the words of Paul, 'I know whom I have believed, and am persuaded that he is able to keep that which I have committed unto him against that day.' As of old, it may be said that 'the preaching of the cross is to them that perish foolishness; but unto us which are saved it is the power of God.' When we remember that the teaching for so many centuries has been that the real individuality of man is material, and that he is dependent on matter for the gratification of his senses and even for the very sustenance of his life, we cannot wonder that so many hesitate to accept the teachings of Christian Science, since this Science demands

the abandonment of all belief in materiality. It
is, nevertheless, true that only as we lose our
belief of life in matter, and our dependence on
matter as a source of sustenance and satisfac-
tion, are we enabled through Christian Science
to grasp the true sense of Life, verifying again
the words of Truth as spoken by Jesus, 'He that
loseth his life for my sake shall find it.' "

IF any Christian Scientists have worried about
Mrs. Eddy's health and strength, that reading
would have ended the worry, could they have
heard it. Among young public speakers there
are few with voices stronger, deeper than the
voice of Mrs. Eddy at eighty-six years of age.
She read the ordinary magazine type without
glasses, as readily as any woman of twenty-five
could do, and with great power of expression
and understanding.

In the course of the afternoon the writer had
three separate talks with Mrs. Eddy. Once, after
the first talk ended and again a second time Mrs.
Eddy said that she had some other things to say.

Aside from the legal matters in which "next
friends" seek to disturb her old age and her

peace, Mrs. Eddy talked chiefly of Christian
Science matters. She was much interested in the
statement made publicly by a granddaughter of
Henry Ward Beecher, who is now a Christian
Science practitioner, that her grandfather if
alive would be a Christian Scientist. The name
of Beecher means of course a great deal to
Mrs. Eddy, who was a young woman at the
height of the great preacher's fame. She spoke
of the work that he did to free the slaves and
said, as though thinking aloud, "Yes, he would
indeed work to free the spirit as he worked to
free the body of the slave."

Mrs. Eddy gave the writer permission to publish a photograph of herself which has not before been seen. Upon this photograph, in the
writer's presence, she wrote her own name as
reproduced with this article. And she wrote also
in the presence of the writer a short note, which
is facsimiled here. This she did at the writer's
request, by way of furnishing visible proof of
her good physical condition. There are certainly
few women of eighty-six that look, talk, think,
or write with greater force and power than does
Mrs. Eddy to-day.

As she said good-by to the writer, rising from

Mary Baker G. Eddy

her chair to hold his hand in both of hers, and to talk with pathetic simplicity and conviction of the good that the visit was to do him, she presented a very beautiful picture of venerable womanhood. Her face, so remarkably young, framed in the beautiful snow-white hair and supported by the delicate, frail, yet erect, body, seemed really the personification of that victory of spirit over matter to which her religion aspires.

Forty years ago, when Mrs. Eddy lived in a garret-like room and told what she believed to be the truth to a world that would not yet listen, stones were thrown through her windows. She spoke of this with sad patience and forgiveness.

To-day, when all the world knows her name, and when many thousands bless that name, Mrs. Eddy finds herself still with enemies eager and energetic against her. They do not throw stones through her windows—that was at the beginning of her teaching. With legal arts and ingenious action they try to control her and the success that she has built up in spite of the early opposition.

The lawyers who oppose her would like to show that Mrs. Eddy is not fit, mentally or physically, to take care of herself or of her fortune, which is considerable. They would like to remove her from her present surroundings, and make her physically subject to the will of others appointed to control her. Success in this effort, in the opinion of the writer, would be shameful, a degradation to all womanhood and old age.

Mrs. Eddy said in her interview, "Young man, I made my money with my pen, just as you do, and I have a right to it." Mrs. Eddy not only has a right to it, but she has the mind to control it.

Those that attack Mrs. Eddy legally, and perhaps sincerely, propose to show that she is "the victim of hallucinations." They will not show this unless American law shall decide that fixed religious belief is a hallucination.

The Turkish minister at Washington, if any court asked him, would say he firmly believes that Mohammed rode up to see God on a galloway named Al Borak, that the intelligent Al Borak bucked and pranced until Mohammed promised him a seat in paradise, that Mohammed studied an interesting angel with seventy thousand heads, "in each head seventy thousand tongues, and each tongue uttered seventy thousand distinct voices at once." The same Turkish gentleman, or any other Mohammedan, would swear to his belief that Mohammed "arriving within two bow-shots of the throne of God, perceived His face covered with seventy thousand veils," and also that "the hand of the Almighty was so cold that, when laid upon his back, it penetrated to the very marrow."

The Turkish minister might testify to these things without being adjudged insane. He has a right to believe in his religion. The ordinary American, not a Christian Scientist, believes that God has so arranged matters that great numbers of His children will be burned for ever and ever in hell fire. Mrs. Eddy believes God has so arranged matters that humanity can cure itself of imagined evils, and escape from all suffering, pain, and "error" through Christian Science teachings.

If the law would refuse to take away the liberty or the property of Christian old ladies because they believe that millions of human beings have been damned from all eternity, it is hard to understand why that law should take away the liberty or the money of Mrs. Eddy because she chooses to believe that eventually nobody will be damned at all.

In substance, Mrs. Eddy's doctrines merely take literally this verse from the fourteenth chapter of John:

"VERILY, verily, I say unto you, He that believeth on me, the works that I do shall he do also; and greater works than these shall he do; because I go unto my Father."—John xiv. 12.

IT is difficult to see why taking literally a statement which this nation as a whole endorses should be construed into a hallucination.

Mrs. Eddy's mind is clear, her health is good for an old lady of eighty-six, her will is strong. She is protected by a very able and absolutely honorable man in the person of her trusted lawyer, General Streeter. She is cared for in her home by women intensely devoted to her. She is able to manage her affairs as much as she may choose to do, and if she were not, no greater crime could be committed against her than to take her from the surroundings that she loves

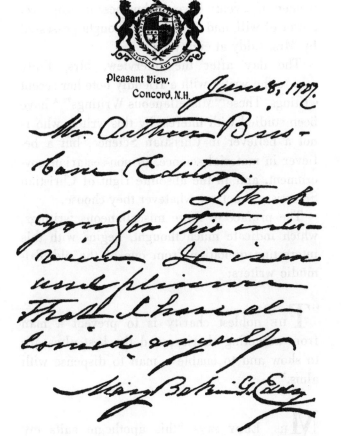

Pleasant View.
Concord, N.H. June 8, 1907.

Mr. Arthur Bris-
bane, Editor.

        I thank
you for this inter-
view. It is an
usual pleasure
that I have al-
lowed myself

        Mary Baker G. Eddy

and the friends that make her happy. Very few women of seventy have the business intelligence, power of will, and clearness of thought possessed by Mrs. Eddy at eighty-six.

The day after the interview, Mrs. Eddy sent to the writer with a friendly note her recent writings. These "Miscellaneous Writings" * have been studied with interest by this writer, who is not a believer in Christian Science, but a believer in material science, in non-sectarian government, and in the absolute right of Christian Scientists to believe whatever they choose.

The preface of these miscellaneous writings, which indicate much thought, begins with this interesting quotation from one of the old Talmudic writers:

"THE noblest charity is to prevent a man from accepting charity; and the best alms are to show and to enable a man to dispense with alms."

MRS. EDDY says "this apothegm suits my sense of doing good."

* Published, 1897.

Mrs. Eddy answers the question, "What do you think of marriage?" as follows:

"THAT it is often convenient, sometimes pleasant, and occasionally a love affair. Marriage is susceptible of many definitions. It sometimes presents the most wretched condition of human existence. To be normal, it must be a union of the affections that tends to lift mortals higher."

IN sending the book Mrs. Eddy marked for the writer some verses by her on page 389. They are reprinted here, because a great number of men and women that love Mrs. Eddy and follow her teachings will like to see the words that evidently express Mrs. Eddy's feelings of consolation at this moment when, in her old age and after a life that has given great happiness and comfort to many, she finds herself the object of an attack from which her years alone should suffice to protect her.

MOTHER'S EVENING PRAYER

O gentle presence, peace and joy and power;
  O Life divine, that owns each waiting hour,
Thou Love that guards the nestling's faltering flight!
  Keep Thou my child on upward wing to-night.

Love is our refuge; only with mine eye
  Can I behold the snare, the pit, the fall:
His habitation high is here, and nigh,
  His arm encircles me, and mine, and all.

O make me glad for every scalding tear,
  For hope deferred, ingratitude, disdain!
Wait, and love more for every hate, and fear
  No ill,—since God is good, and loss is gain.

Beneath the shadow of His mighty wing;
  In that sweet secret of the narrow way,
Seeking and finding, with the angels sing:
  "Lo, I am with you alway,"—watch and pray.

No snare, no fowler, pestilence or pain;
  No night drops down upon the troubled breast,
When heaven's aftersmile earth's tear-drops gain,
  And mother finds her home and heavenly rest.

CPSIA information can be obtained at www.ICGtesting.com
Printed in the USA
BVOW08s0128130614

356277BV00007B/65/P